Not Just A Rib

Understanding
The Purpose and Power of
Wife-Mother-Woman

By

Lenora C. Yarbrough

Edited by
Claude R. Royston

BK Royston Publishing, LLC
Jeffersonville, IN

BK Royston Publishing

P. O. Box 4321

Jeffersonville, IN 47131

502-802-5385

http://bkroystonpublishing.com

bkroystonpublishing@gmail.com

Published by: BK Royston Publishing LLC
Cover: CustomWebchoice.com
Layout by: BK Royston Publishing LLC

ISBN-13: 978-0615944531

ISBN-10: 0615944531

Printed in the United States of America

Table of Contents

DEDICATION

To my husband Edward Louis Yarbrough who was a confidant, an advisor and main support for 30 years of marriage. (July 15, 1950-January 14, 2006)

To my sisters Judith, Marian, Carol Ann and my dear departed Maurice, from whom I received valuable, wanted and unwanted advice on love, life and the raising of successful children. To the many late telephone calls, the early morning prayers and the relentless hours of conversation on the blessings and woes of motherhood.

To my four sons; Edward Jr, Ean, Evan and Eric. To whom I've had the joy of being mother, counselor, intercessor, mediator and who I have had the pleasure of receiving much love from. I thank God for the patience and the knowledge to help bring them to the men of integrity they are today. "To God be the glory".

To my five special, unique, diamonds; Desaray, Gabrielle, James, Jalen and Li'son, to whom God has enabled me to be their mother through adoption. My prayer-life has evolved to another realm, however, I still have had dark circles underneath the eyes,-sore knees and bouts of insomnia. I love you with the love only God can give.

And finally, to the women of Fountain of Faith Christian Center from which the strength and support comes in immeasurable amounts of love that abounds in abundant doses, to the; mothers, widows, divorced and those who are surrogates. I applaud you for your wisdom and prayers.

INTRODUCTION

It is extremely difficult to be a strong woman. Many of us are struggling to discover who we are and where we stand with our families, our communities, jobs and even our walk with God. Day after day we ask ourselves "For what purpose am I here? What can I do to feel valuable, accepted and praised?" These ongoing questions plague women and we stop trying to find answers. That's only because we except misery, defeat, depression and mere existence. We fail to receive the revelation of who we are in the sight of God.

There's a lot to be said in this day and time about the role of a female, the one we call Woman. She has an awesome responsibility and is most often over looked and underestimated for the extra ordinary tasks she performs in everyday life. A Woman, Mother, Intercessor, Peacemaker, Interpreter are just few of thc names that are spiritual roles we take on daily. We don't understand why she (Woman) evolves in these areas, but as you read this book I promise, that the revelation will come as it came to me. We are called, appointed, and anointed to take on the responsibility as we grow in Christ and in the Word of God. I would also like to emphasize that if you don't *seek*, you won't *find*.

I'm not only talking about going after natural things like money, men, or sexual gratification, but this is why so many past efforts on behalf of women have fallen short of success. Tangible things!

This book will open your eyes to the spiritual being of women. Yes, you are a spiritual being who was created from a rib, out of a man, by God. (Gen. 1:26) So for all the ladies reading this get ready, you're not <u>just</u> a RIB!!

Alert-Alert-Alert

April 17, 2004

I am rushing my husband Edward to the emergency room. It may be another heart attack. "God forbid!" Everyone intercessors, friends and loved ones are all praying for him.

April 18, 2004. 10:00 a.m.

I am here at Norton's Hospital and our worries were confirmed. It was another heart attack. He had suffered one before in 2002. Right now he is looking well and talking. God is good!!

April 23, 2004. 12 noon

I was talking to Edward on the phone while he was eating. He was sounding so good. Suddenly he began to cough and make choking sounds. I arrived at the hospital and the doctors informed me that he had a stroke which affected his right side and his speech.

May, June, July 2004

My husband has been admitted to his second nursing home because the first proved to be substandard. There was a case of neglect and we saw it very necessary to remove him from that facility.

He had been back and forth from the hospital to the dialysis back to the nursing home. This caused him to become very weak and he-subsequently gave up his fight on January 14, 2006 and went to sleep in the Lord.

Chapter One
And the Rib Which GOD Made

Then the rib which the Lord God had taken from man He made into a woman, and He brought her to the man. (Gen. 2:22) NKJV

Alright church, open your bibles to Genesis 2:22.

How many times have we read that scripture, heard it over the pulpit or even heard it over and over in our own minds? Too numerous to remember, and yet this scripture is taken out of context and women are manipulated, abused, and confused.

All too often, I can remember listening and receiving all that was told to me by men, male pastors, teachers and others in authority. I had never read it for myself. I also took it as truth and never questioned any of it. "This is your place. The rib, right beside the man." Now, some would say "behind man", which is another chapter, but beside her (man) I can live with.

Can you imagine what Eve was thinking when she was given to Adam? Can you imagine what Adam saw when he looked at her? She was naked! WOW! This was good because innocence abounded and they saw each other through God's eyes. Adam and Eve were made in the image and likeness of God, spiritual and pure. Eve was created from Adam's side and destined to be at his side.

Well, we all know that story; God took the man and put him in the Garden of Eden to cultivate it, and God told him he could eat of every tree, but of the tree of Knowledge of Good and Evil, the man shall not eat or he will die. Now Eve had not been created yet, and God was laying down the rules to Adam. As the story goes, Eve was created and was then deceived by the devil and they were immediately ostracized and cut off from the spiritual blessing God intended for them to have. What started out to be a great love story, ended in damnation and deception!

Wouldn't it be fantastic if all our dreams, wishes and desires appeared before our eyes just by thinking about them? She'd have the perfect mate, house, children, and more than enough money to live large. But that's not the way God planned for us to live. "Delight yourself also in the Lord, and he will give you the desires of your heart." (Psalm 37:4) It would be better for you to spend weeks reading and studying God's Word before you even form your prayer, than to just pray and assume it is God's will. In Eccl 5:2 we find this admonition; "Be not rash with thy mouth, and let not thine heart be hasty to utter anything before God: for God is in heaven, and thou upon earth: therefore let thy words be few KJV." Then in Psalm 37:7a we read, "Rest in the Lord and wait patiently for him.." The Hebrew translation says, "To be silent to the Lord." Sometimes we do too much asking, pleading, and praying or we pray the wrong prayer at the wrong time.

I didn't know this when I was a young adult. I just assumed that God would grant my every wish and desire. I didn't have a prayer life; only when I had a problem or wanted something. I would pray or beg God to grant my request.

I had just come out of a failed relationship and engagement, and now that I realize and think about it; I had a mental breakdown. He (ex-fiancé) had decided to postpone the wedding weeks before the event. Had I not seen his car parked at our clergy's house (which was across the street from my house) all day, I would have never found out about the cancelation. Long story short, the wedding was cancelled, and I remained engaged for 2 years. During that time I tried to make our relationship better; but it wasn't meant to be. I see the mistakes now that we made then. We never prayed. Read the Word, or even went for counseling. I just hoped for the best. I was the type that kept everything inside. I was too afraid of hurting the other person and letting my true feelings out. I tried to change myself for him (fiancé).

I began to read my Bible, and I remember praying one Saturday night and asking God to help me through this ordeal. I remember the Holy Spirit saying that I was not alone, and that this wasn't my portion in life to be depressed and unhappy. That very night I had a dream. In this dream, I was coming down the aisle to meet my (fiancé), let's call him Adam. There were no decorations in the church! I immediately got Adam's attention and mouthed to him, "Where are the decorations?" He simply shrugged his shoulders and mouthed back, "I don't know." I continued to walk down the aisle. When I came to another halt, I realized that there was no photographer. I got his attention again and mouthed, "Where is the photographer?" Adam once again shrugged his shoulders and said, "I don't know." Well, by this time I was ready to turn around and leave. As the groom was to take the hand of the bride when she completed her walk down the aisle, I looked again, at what I expected to be Adam. I then came face to face with Edward (my husband now). By the way, I had never seen or met this man ever in life until I saw him in my dream. Screaming, I awakened to an uncomfortable shaking and profuse perspiring. What was that dream all about? What was God trying to tell me? These questions shot through my head as I tried to make some sense of it all. There was an older sister of the church, Sis Mary Levels, who was my spiritual mother whom I confided in quite often. This night I called her and relayed to her everything that I saw in my dream. She asked me the very same questions that I had asked myself. After much thought and consideration, the Holy Spirit began to reveal to me what my dream exactly meant.

This is what the Holy Spirit revealed to me. The undecorated church and the absence of the photographer was a sign of Adam's heart. He was not fully persuaded or in the love frame of mind for marriage. He just didn't care. We were headed for disaster if we united in Holy Matrimony and would more than likely end up in divorce court.

That night I made a big decision that surprisingly enough wasn't difficult to make at all, because the Holy Spirit had told me what to say and do. The next morning, Sunday, it was my Sunday to usher. Adam walked into the church and I greeted him at the door and asked to speak to him privately outside. I told him that I was led to do this, and I give him back his ring. I also explained to him that marriage to each other was a big mistake and that neither one of us had the type of love that would survive in a real marriage. He agreed without any argument which really puzzled me afterwards, now that I think about it. I handed him his ring, and he accepted it with a thanks and a smile. Boy was he "broken up!"

I learned later that the night I had my dream, Adam was at a party talking to another woman who later became his wife. What a turn of events!!

The next six months went like a blur. I dated a couple of brothers. -That turned out to be disastrous. I had a check list of the characteristics that I wanted my husband to possess;

1) He had to be mannerable. You know girls, he must open the car door and let you in first.
2) Compliment you whenever the opportunity presents itself.
3) Pay for all dates!!!
4) Note: this is very important. A brother shouldn't ask a sister out on a date and take her over to his sister's house for a dinner that consists of brown beans and corn bread. PAH-LE-ASE!!!!

Brothers need to know that when they ask a sister out they should make sure that his car is not a death trap. He ought not get in first and reach over and open the door for you! But the biggest cardinal sin a brother can commit is to compliment another sister in front of you! These are just a few incidents I went through before I met the *man of my dreams.*

It was a Saturday night and I was once again ushering during a huge conference held at our church. I remember that I was tremendously thirsty and as I approached the water fountain I bumped into Edward, who was finishing his drink of water. Our eyes met and we just gazed at each other for a brief moment. I excused myself and went back into church, but I couldn't get him out of my mind.

I went home that night and immediately called Sister May and told her about him. She began to tell me of a brother who had just been "born again." He had been in the Air Force and spent four years in Germany. She continued to tell me that he had a German accent, was very mannerly, loved the Lord, and oh yeah, he's also "looking for a wife."

Oh snap!! The antennas had gone up ladies!!! You see, I said that I wasn't looking for a husband but my heart felt differently. It happened again only on Sunday evening after services, my thirst got the best of me, and as I drank from the water fountain, he came up behind me and spoke softly with a German accent, "I didn't have dinner today, would you like to join me?" I thought that I was well, I couldn't tell you what I thought, but I know that voice with the German accent melted every barrier. I joined him for dinner that day and it turned into many more dinner and occasions. Until one day, he asked me to marry him and I said, yes! Plans began and excitement was in full swing to prepare for the blessed event, our wedding day.

The sanctuary was arranged in red and white carnations and huge satin bows. Each bow represented a reserved section. This was an indication of the difference between where the family members would sit and where the visitors seating would begin. My mother and mother in-law to be were in the church's ladies lounge awaiting my arrival. These two special women to me and my future husband would assist me in getting dressed for the blessed occasion. My other sisters Marian, Maurice and Judith were busy supervising guests, taking care of the reception's last minute details, and making sure that everyone in the wedding party was present and accounted for.

The ceremony went without incident. Only after we were pronounced man and wife did I go down the aisle whispering loudly "tonight-tonight-tonight!" There were chuckles in the audience with the look of embarrassment on my mother's face, I hugged my husband tightly and whispered in his ear, "for always and forever."

Chapter Two
Can we really HAVE what we Say?

I have always said to myself and others that I was going to have four sons. It was my foremost desire for years and years. Every time the subject of children came up, I mentioned the four sons that I had confessed for years. People either laughed and/or agreed with me. Some gazed mysteriously out of the corner of their eyes, but it was my family that questioned my sanity.

Well in 1975 there were many, many weddings. All or most of the (wives) were already pregnant three months later, except me. Girls, we were trying everything, every position, every time of the day, every exotic food (aphrodisiacs) and every cream! The harder we tried the more we failed and it was beginning to affect me emotionally. Now Edward, on the other hand, was a little worn out, but was enjoying the ride. He never complained, in fact, he was compassionate, understanding and very concerned. He was my rock!

To ease the tension and to rid ourselves of the anxiety of the situation, we went on a mini vacation for a few days to Ohio. We were having a fabulous time until I saw about four or five pregnant women walking around. That experience brought the feelings back to the surface again. I got over it and when we returned home I quickly found out I was three days late with my period. Now concerning periods, I'm regular like clockwork, never late always on time. But much to my surprise I was late, happy, elated and overjoyed!

Edward Louis Yarbrough Jr. weighed in at 5.7 pounds and 21½ inches, was born in February of 1977. He was overdue and during delivery he had a bowel movement which could've caused some serious seizure problems, but the Lord was present so that just wasn't gonna' happen.

During the ride home from the hospital, I said that I wished that Edward, (whom we now call Twinkie) and who resembles the long thin, edible delight full of cream filling, had a brother. Now, remember I have been continuously confessing these things (Mark 11:24) not knowing I had spoken them into existence. Two and half months after the birth of Edward Jr. I found out I was pregnant with Ean Leonard, my second. It was a wonderful pregnancy, although not always comfortable, you know carrying one in your belly and one on your hip. Ean entered the world on February 1st, 1978. Now Edward is eleven and half months old and not walking too well and not even a year old yet. Yes ladies, I know what you're probably thinking with one toddler and an infant, temporary insanity or was she nuts? No, just in love.

Let me explain this to you. At this time I was worshiping at a traditional Pentecostal Church where we operated from a doctrine of *don'ts*;

1) Don't drink
2) Don't smoke
3) Don't dance
4) Don't use birth control (women were put here to replenish the earth)
5) Don't commit adultery

....and the list goes on. I was an obedient soul, listening and obeying everything that was told to me by the elders (men). Now please understand! Through this obedience, I was taught patience, to read and study the Word myself. The experience of studying enabled me to establish a closer relationship with God.

About seventeen months later we were blessed with the arrival of my third son (Evan). He was a quick birth, healthy and vibrant. God is very faithful in his word. You see, all these years I had been confessing a desire for children and I believed it, not knowing that I had quickened that portion of scripture in Mark 11:24. ".....What things so ever you desire, when you pray, believe that you will receive them and you shall have them." KJV Confession is the key.

Seventeen months later after the birth of Evan we were blessed a fourth time with the birth of Eric. He was number four, the last of our biological sons!

As time went on they began to grow up and develop their own unique personalities. Every day was a challenge and an adventure for all of us. Sitting at the table was one of the times I loved most about being with my loves. They were happy, creative and just *joys*. You know the old cliché "boys will be boys!" That included the insects found in the pockets of dirty laundry. The boys would put olive oil on the sledding board so that the poor innocent cat could slide down faster than a speeding bullet. The silent farts at the dinner table. The unspoken code that brings forth the uncontrollable laughter were enjoyable, but that can pick at your last nerve! Motherhood gotta' love it with its demands, the highs, the lows and even the in-betweens.

When my sons were in the middle of elementary school age, it was then that my prayer life became a very intricate tool. -That was very much needed to raise my boys. They became challenging asking potent questions like; "how do babies come out? What street does God live on? Do people run by batteries?" I tried to answer them with God's help and the best way I knew. Of course, they observed and questioned their mom and dad's relationship and interaction with each other. Let me put this in simpler terms. One night when we thought they were in a deep sleep, we were in the throes of passion and Edward got excited screaming "O baby, O baby, O baby!" Well could they sleep soundly through the 'O babies?' No. Down the short hallway came the voices of 4, half sleep boys shouting, "momma, daddy what are ya'll doing!? Are ya'll wrestling again? Did daddy win mama? Can we come in?" I was suddenly filled with utter embarrassment, with my hands up to my mouth, trying to stifle the heavy breathing brought on by the vigorous activity of the night, whereas my husband was finding utter enjoyment at the questions on the other side of the door.

He was laughing and crying at the same time. That made me angry watching him get his jollies from my discomfort. It took about five minutes to compose ourselves. We then opened the door and reassured them that mom and dad are finished with their wrestling and finally convinced them to go back to bed. The next morning, there were mysterious looks along with giggling and private whispers. And I, in the meantime, was hovered over the stove trying to hide the still embarrassed, flush of last night's events.

As time went on, they developed their own character, likes, dislikes and individuality. Eric was becoming a joker, an experimenter, and loved that urge to discover new things. The boy loved to ask questions, no matter how utterly, ridiculous, or preposterous. Evan was developing into an intellect, artist and perfectionist. He loved to try new things and had a strange affection for hats. Ean, on the other hand, was a strange bird growing up. He never said much but was body in action. He was a protector, the go between and the enforcer. I'm reminded of an incident that happened at our church. I was working in the nursery during the service, and next door there was what we called the toddler room, for the children who could walk and get around on their own. My sister in-law Jean was volunteering with those toddlers. Well, to make a long story short, one of the toddlers (being a toddler) hit my oldest son, Edward Jr. and Edward, Jr. began to cry. Ean immediately cried out "Twinkie (Edward's nickname) are you ok? Did he hurt you? I will get him for you!" he commenced to deliver judgment on that little fella' and so there were two in tears. Edward Jr., my firstborn, was humble, quite spoken, and obedient. He battled with an inner turmoil. He touched my heart very deeply and this drove me into a deeper relationship with God. This relationship allowed me to pray and see actual manifestation of my prayers. That is when the Holy Spirit began to reveal to me that I must become an intercessor, mediator, covenant maker, prayer warrior and a curse breaker!

Chapter Three
Enough is Enough

As previously stated, Edward Louis Yarbrough Jr. came into this world at five pounds seven ounces, two and a half inches long and was two weeks over due. The doctor was very concerned during the delivery because Edward had a bowel movement while he was still in the womb. But mercy prevailed and all was well. Praise the Lord!

He grew into a very fine young man. He was a man of few words, always eager to please, but something was not right. You know mothers, that feeling you have when you have sensed that something is not adding up. Uncertainty and fear had set in. Then questions arose that I didn't want to ask myself. Is he an alcoholic? Is he on drugs? Is he gay? Is he sexually active? Edward would come home from school and just go straight to his room. My other sons would be playing, teasing each other and just doing the male bonding thing.

I began to ask the Lord, “What is going on with my son?” And with that same breath I told the Devil, “You can’t have him!”

On one occasion, he got into an argument with one of his brothers. It had become pretty heated, and Edward went into his room and slammed the door. His brothers were pretty upset and concerned, because they saw Edward take a knife into the room with him. When I got to Edward’s room, he was standing facing his bed with the knife pointed toward his stomach. I slowly walked in and began to speak softly and quietly to a sobbing, emotional young man. “I’ll do it, I’ll do it, and just let me go” he screamed between the sobs. I immediately grabbed the knife and his brothers secured him in their arms.

My first born was in my arms. I worked and prayed and he confided to me that the spirit of low self-esteem wanted to consume him. But it had to come through me first! He felt so helpless, with his fragile, thin body he confessed all the suicidal thoughts that he had had for months. He imagined that he was ugly, nobody wanted to be his friend, and that he wasn't goin' to be anything. I sat there, stunned, numbed and not believing my ears. Then the anger sat in. You see, the Word declares that the Devil is a liar and the father of all lies. He (Devil) had lied to my son. He had hung onto these negative thoughts and ideas for months. Now mothers, here's where the fight comes in. When I had my first born, I dedicated him to God for His services. I saw the enemy trying to destroy him. I wasn't going to let that happen. Arm yourself mothers!! It was time to go to war. I began to take the authority that was given to me by the Lord. "The kingdom of Heaven suffered violence: and the violent take it by force." Matt 11:12 KJV I held him tightly to my bosom and spoke the Word over him. "You are above and not beneath, you are a righteous mighty young man of God, you will be victorious, and you are highly favored of God." I asked him, who was he going to believe, the voice of Satan, or the written Word of God?

It's still amazing to me that the very Word of God quenches that negative atmosphere when it's spoken in faith! "So shall they (demons) fear the name of the Lord from the west, and his glory from the rising of the sun? When the enemy (Devil) shall come in like a flood, the spirit of the Lord shall lift up a standard against him." Isa 59:19 KJV

He began to read and study the Word as never before, and the Word began to transform, comfort him and give him confidence, self-esteem and more importantly, protected him during a tour of duty in Iraq and back home safely. God is faithful!!

Now, I'm very family oriented. My mother and father blessed me to be one out of eight children. There were three sets of twins and two singles. My father would always tease us and say “Your mom was mad because she didn’t make the news reel.” (You know back in the day 1940’s as it was called). I was blessed to have a twin brother, Leonard. He was the rambunctious one. I am the meek and sweet one. Well, as time went on, in 1952 Leonard was stricken with crippling polio and thus began his journey apart from me.

I remember watching him through the hospital window one cold Christmas eve as he waved back at us with tear stained eyes and bewilderment. My parents, especially mom, took on this burden with love as their ammunition. They were courageous and relentless. Mom would teach us the exercises they taught her at the hospital; and every night before bedtime she would lay him on our kitchen table and begin the torture - filled, rigors of muscle stretches, knee bends, and sit ups. I could hear his painful screams and pleadings for her to stop; but she would say softly, "I love you baby, but mama has to do this." That went on, and on and on.

We made it through high school together! By then he had made a name for himself as being the class clown, notorious with the ladies and being my protector. That included threats to any males that might possibly be interested in me. Now, most of you would say that's a good thing, but when the love-notes and little tokens of fondness are intercepted and opened, that's where I drew the line. His days of knight ship were over.

Now don't get me wrong, Leonard's heart was always in the right place, especially when it came to the Civil Rights movement. Dr. Martin Luther King, Jr. would be in town; and guess who would be the one to chauffer him? You're right! When several black students were arrested during the sit-ins and demonstrations downtown, who was seen waving to the camera as the policemen held one of his crutches and lifted him into the patty wagon with the rest of the demonstrators? Right again. He loved living life without boundaries or having to answer to anyone, which is why he chose the drug and alcohol scene.

I don't know if someone introduced him to drugs or he was just stuck on stupid and/or inquisitive, but he spiraled into a dangerous addictive life which almost got him killed. At this time in his life he had gone through two wives and he had five children and was living with a user.

It was a Wednesday evening and I had received a call from my oldest brother saying that Leonard and his friend were missing. We were all worried about him because of his lifestyle. I told my brother that I would pray and that they would be back home Friday. Now, I didn't know where that came from but, I do know that when I prayed that afternoon, angels were released to protect and bring them home safely. Jesus said, " For verily I say unto you, That whosoever shall say unto this mountain, Be thou removed, and be thou cast into the sea; and shall not doubt in his heart, but shall believe that those things which he saith shall come to pass;

he shall have whatsoever he saith." Mark 11:23 KJV

Friday afternoon came and my brother called me. I still remember the conversation we had. "Hey sis, I hear that you prayed us home." "Yeah, and you know that I saw you two in the Spirit and you were in grave danger."

"You're right, they (drug dealers) were going to kill us, and for no reason they said, no, we'll just let them go." I heard the crying in his voice, "You know Nonnie, I knew that you were praying for me because I felt a safe presence and I knew we were goin' to be alright."

For the drug and alcohol addicts who read this book: Drugs are like hooks in the mouth of a fish. "As the hook goes, so goes the fish." -Take the hook out of your mouth!! How? Sit down, clear your mind and let the Holy Spirit minister to you! How do I know it's the Holy Spirit? Will the Holy Spirit tell you to go out and get high NO! Will the Holy Spirit tell you to do whatever to get your high? NO!

This is the voice that comes to you and says that you

need help and that God is the answer. Get to someone that you know can pray and lead you to Christ. Do It Now!!

Prayer of Salvation

Lord, I know that I am a sinner.

Right now I confess my sins, and I renounce Satan as my Lord.

I accept you Jesus as my Lord and my Savior.

I believe that you died for my sins and went to hell, rose again and I know you are seated on the right hand of God, forever praying for me. I believe I am saved now and I am a new creation in Christ Jesus. Amen.

Chapter Four
Train Up A Child

What I've learned from raising my four sons is that parenting_is not for cowards; or my sons would say not for "punks!" It's demanding; and scary. Scary in the sense that you don't know what you're doing and you don't want them to end up like that certain relative(s) that every family hides. Of course you want the best for them without spoiling them, and then on the other hand you want to be firm without being abusive. You want to show them what to do and how to do it. You also want them to be disciplined and not out of control.

It makes a huge difference when both parents are believers (Christians). The obstacles of life present a challenge. And then there are *soul-ties* and *generational curses*. Let me explain. Soul ties are those sprits that have attached themselves to us as we were growing up. The soul ties can come as early as 'in the womb.' These soul ties can be influences from people, relatives that we like or dislike. There are habits that develop into real soul ties that were introduced from previous generations.

For example: Grandpa has dipped snuff or chewing tobacco for years and he's as strong as an ox. Uncle John-John says there's nothing wrong with having four girlfriends and a wife. Grandma attends church regularly, sits on the Mother's board and serves on the Willing-To-fry-Chicken Committee whereas; Uncle John-John is the head Deacon and leads the prayer every Sunday morning. They seem to be good spiritual people. Our sons and daughters, are exposed to this concept of life and accept it. Generational curses, on the other hand, go much deeper. "My grandmother was on welfare, my mother was on welfare, and now it's my turn." I don't see anything wrong with that. "The government owes me." "They done kept us down for hundreds of years, now they got to pay!" Another example:

cousin Ce-Ce had cancer and died at 42, her mother died before her at 40 and her two sisters after her at 41. “So, child I think you better get yo' house in order, 'cause, how old is you? 39! You got about 1 or 2 years 'fore you be eatin’ dirt.” Do these words sound familiar? Our ancestors had a lot to contend with, but now the light has come!!

The Word of God says in Ephesians 6:12 “For we wrestle not against flesh and blood, but against principalities against powers, against the rulers of darkness of this world, against spiritual wickedness in the high places.” Our flesh is not saved, so therefore there is that battle between our flesh and the spirit. Now let me back up a little. In order to be victorious in a battle we first must be *in* Christ. "That if thou shalt confess with thy mouth the Lord Jesus, and shalt believe in thine heart that God hath raised him from the dead, thou shalt be saved.

For with the heart man believeth unto righteousness; and with the mouth confession is made unto salvation." Romans 10:9,10 KJV

There's a difference in *knowing of Him* and having a *relationship* with Him. I can't imagine waking up in the morning and not acknowledging the Creator. Thanking him for breath, protection while I slept, sight, hearing, and mobility. It is good to give thanks. You have made the sinners confession, and now that you are saved and know of Him, it's time to begin a relationship with him. Faith filled words will put you over. Fear filled words will defeat you. Words are the most powerful things in the universe. Start confessing the Word- but in order to confess the Word, you must read the Word. Read: Mark 9:23/Matthew 17:20/Mark 11:22-24/ John 14:12/ Romans 10:17. To you men, converts, sons, daughters, fathers and especially *mothers*, these scriptures will start your walk with Lord. It will make faith your lifestyle. Now comes the harder part "To Adopt or Not To Adopt" that was the question!!

Our four sons are a joy; never a dull moment. They are funny, inquisitive, and of course, every parent thinks intelligent ranks up there with #1. But, something is missing. Let's say it was variety. My husband wanted more females in the house, besides the cats and myself.

He had told me some months before he had a dream that we were going to become parents of two daughters. My reaction was screaming of course, "I'm not having any more babies!"

Now that I have calmed down; Edward in his sultry voice, tells me that in his dream we had two little girls as the dream goes on, he explains that these two females have been adopted by us and we were *so* happy. Well, when you put it like that, who am I to argue?

We called the Foster-Care office and got signed up to take the classes immediately. Every Monday for about seven weeks we were at the meetings prompt and ready to get out of it, *what we were supposed to*! Look, let me explain. We were told that these meetings were counter-productive that they tell parents how to be parents, the "What to and what not to do, rules–rules–rules on the do's and don'ts" of parenting. Of course we *knew* how to parent; but these were a certain breed of kid, from different backgrounds and circumstances. We were in for the ride of our lives. God had prepared us.

After we had gone through the rigorous training, the home evaluation, where they come and assess your home, interview your children that live there, and talk to your close relatives, we were approved. Then came the waiting game. You wait for a child or sibling groups to become available. Months had gone by and no kid. We called, the only response was, "Mr. and Mrs. Yarbrough we have you on the active list, and as soon as a child becomes available, we'll give you a call."

One month later, July, we received a call asking us if we would be interested in keeping two little boys while their foster parents were on vacation for two weeks. This was called the Respite Program where foster families need a break, they pay another foster family to babysit, for the weekend or for vacation proposes.

Not long after that experience, we were called and asked to take a toddler who was 21 months and who had been abandoned by her mother in January of 1991. I was burying my mother who had passed away of breast cancer. My family was adamant! “Don’t take that child, you need some peace right now; a kid is the last thing you need!” I called my husband at work, and being the caring person that he was, he said “Honey, take the baby.” and that began our journey with my fine diamonds. That was Desaray. Seven months later we found out that Desaray’s mother was pregnant again and didn’t know when the baby was due because she had not been to the doctor for a prenatal check-up. In fact she never went for any prenatal check-up which is why she delivered Gabrielle prematurely that following February of "1992." It was an experience having two girls in the household, other than myself and Mai Ling, my Siamese cat. Thusly, the adventures began.

Not long after the girls, we were blessed to acquire three more sons that have given us joy beyond belief. First was Jalen who was born in February, not long after Jalen, then came James, born in the same year, actually on St. Patrick Day. I called him my little black leprechaun. Rounding up the bunch was Li'son, who has reaped the benefit of being spoiled by everyone. There you have it, my five pearls, and assorted nuts, whatever you want to call them. They were ours, bought and paid for, and we never looked back to what ifs, should haves or if things were different. This was God's plan, yeah and amen. From that time on we knew we were getting another child because I would have dreams about a kid and my husband would hear a baby crying.

How cool was that? That's what I call "Divine Intervention." We enjoyed James to the fullest. He was the softest, cuddly and sweet dispositional baby and toddler, until about five years old. By then the cuddliness had gotten old, and he was school age.

My husband and I longed for another small bundle right out of the oven. We called the Cabinet at foster care and inquired about another child, preferably infant preferably male. In two months, we received a call from two workers approximately 8:45 am, who were in the process of just discharging a 2 day old black infant from the hospital around 9:15 am. Of course we said yes and of course I was ecstatically getting dressed to make a mad dash to the hospital! Too late!! At 9:35 a.m. they were ringing my door bell with a large, suitcase and baby. Li'son entered our lives with a vengeance. He did everything early, walking at 9 months, talking at one year. At age seven, he's still a blessed wonder, fearfully and wondrously made: he has impacted our lives just with his presence.

Children are a blessing from God whether planned or not. And the difficultly about parenting is that kids don't come with instructions. We as parents tend to raise our children the way were raised, the way we think is the right way; just one day at a time, or just experimenting by the book. Either way, it's a serious position and very scary at times, knowing that you have been entrusted with the tiny human to raise, to be a perfectly, great individual.

After raising my four biological sons, it still stands to reason that training up a child is a God thing. The child should be God centered and God focused. (Prov. 22:6) Training up a child the way he should go, and when he is old, he will not depart from it. Now, this scripture "simply train" means to make way for *them to do and not just ask them to* go a specific path. When doing it God's way that means teaching them to be: loving, obedient and honest. These attitudes are attainable only when he or she is raised in the Lord. It's going to take prayer and patience on your part; and mostly studying the Word of the Lord. There are a lot of books written by successful Christian parents who have raised extraordinary children. You can do it! Let's raise a generation of Joshuas.

Chapter Five
Dreams and Visions
(Decisions, decisions, decisions)

Now that my child bearing days were over, and God had blessed us with the desires of our hearts which were our four sons, we had to make a very important decision. To adopt, or not to adopt.

After our sons were born, my husband, somehow, got the urge to have more females in the house. Look, don't get me wrong, my husband loved our sons but, with he's exact words "a home is not complete without both genders." That got us thinking, and we decided to go into Foster Care.

It was an easy decision because we both loved kids, and the thought of having two little girls in the house was just too good for words.

My husband and I took it very seriously when it came to being Foster parents, and eventually adoption. We were in constant prayer asking the Lord, if this was the right decision.

Yes, the answer was yes. I remember clearly one memory before my husband went off to work; he informed me that he had heard a baby crying. But we had no babies in the house at the time. But we did ask for a baby at one Foster Care interview. I can now understand why I didn't get upset; I had a dream the night before about a baby. Well, that was our confirmation, and the last three children, the boys, were revealed to us the very same way.

It didn't take long to fill out the paper work and also go through six weeks of training. You know, the dos and don'ts placed on you by the state on how to raise committed children.

The training was long and stressful but we received important information. We met several foster parents who had good experiences with foster care. We also met other foster parents who, well, let's just say they didn't have those words of encouragement that the others brought to the table.

January 6, 1992 is a day I won't forget. For one, I was burying my mother the very next day, and it was the day that our first daughter, Desaray Valentine was handed to us through the front door by some shabby little man with a Kroger bag in his hand. Desary, at 14 months old reached out for me as her delivery man handed me her belongings. I carried her into the kitchen where my four sons greeted her with smiles and laughter. As I held her in my lap, I asked my sons what we should have for dinner and they all shouted their orders. And Desaray heard one of her favorite words, pizza. She immediately repeated pizza in her small voice. So pizza it was!!

During the foster care experience you are asked if you want to meet or get to know the biological family. Of course, my husband, being the gentle heart that he was, said yes. A meeting with the mother was set up at the L&N

building (Foster Care Head Quarters) and there we began our journey both happy and sad.

There were many conversations about her daughter, Desary. Already my family and I had come to love her tremendously. She was a challenge and also a joy. But that joy quickly turned into an, 'oh, oh.' Her mother informed us that she was pregnant again and didn't know the due date or if this unborn child would be healthy; and the biggest bomb shell of all, she had no idea who the father was. The social worker passed on this news to us about the pregnancy. We were then asked if we would be interested in taking on an infant also; since we were at that time in the process of termination of rights of the mother and starting the adoption procedure.

It was yes! It was a hands down decision for my husband and me. He loved the idea of a toddler and newborn in the house. There were times spent in prayer and endless conversations with our sons. Well, what could I say?

They were all on board and accepted the oncoming responsibilities that came along with our decision to adopt.

In the months that led up to the girl's adoption, their mother was having some difficulties with the turn of events and therefore, she began to fight to get custody. Now, she had just given birth to the most beautiful gray eyed little girl, who was six pounds and three ounces. Introducing Gabrielle Antoinette!!

The girl's mother had no means of income, no place to stay and she also had a problem with alcohol. She had been a transient most of her young adult life. That meant that she never had a home, but went house to house staying with those who would let her stay there for a while.

Well, I'm sad to say that when the termination hearing came around, she didn't show up, and she also had not improved her living conditions; on the other hand she didn't have to show up. We basically didn't have to show up; which I'm glad that we were not required to do so. The termination judgment was handed down by the judge. The baby's mother was highly upset and threatened everyone.

One year later, we were standing before the judge, Desaray, Gabrielle, Edward Sr. and myself, affirming that we were who we said we were and that we promised to care for these two precious girls with all the godly love we have within us! It was such a celebration; my four sons Edward Jr, Ean, Evan and Eric; my extended family and many friends and co-workers were all there. Now we are eight, but we have three more to go. Brace – Yourself!!!

It wasn't long before my other three gems came into our lives. Like I previously said, I would have a dream about the child, and my husband would hear a baby crying. We got James and Jalen a month apart. Jalen's birthday is February the 24th and James's on March 17th, St. Patrick's Day. I call him my 'little black leprechaun.'

When James and Jalen became old enough to sit up; we had two babies to carry on one hip. It was a challenge, because it was like having twins, but it was rewarding. They grew to be humble and kind toward one another, the way brothers should be.

Six years passed by and one Thursday morning around 8:40 a.m., we received a call about a two day old infant boy that they wanted to place with us. They wanted us to be there by nine o'clock, but obviously that was impossible. Around 9:15 the doorbell rang and the social worker was there on my porch with an armload of blankets. He was as precious as can be. Weighing in at six pounds and two ounces, at two days old, we welcomed little Li'son with open arms.

Chapter Six
From the book of momma one and one

Ladies, sometimes you go through trials; you have happy experiences, you receive devastating news, but yet you learn valuable life lessons that you can't ignore. Somewhere in your '*Knowah*' you know what you know what you know.

There's no debate, no second guessing. You just know!!

Well, I'm just gonna' jump right in. This chapter is going to be disturbing to some, but, enlightening to others.

My husband Edward had a very quiet and gentle spirit. He loved his family, and at the beginning of our marriage, he became a faithful husband and father, and a doting son. In other words, as the saying goes, he was a mamma's boy. Now, some of you would define him as one who was at his mother's beckon call; but not Edward. You see, his father abandoned the family (of seven boys and one girl) when he was five years of age. Edward vowed that he would support the family at any cost. He was true to his word. He failed two grades in high school because he felt the need to get a job and help support his mom and the other siblings that were living at home. As a result, he graduated from Central High School two years late. After graduation, he immediately joined the Air Force and was stationed at Rhein Main Air Force Base in Frankfort, Germany for four years.

The Lord kept him safe and he was honorably discharged to come home to me! Living with Edward, life was sweet. He was focused and down to earth. He was one who loved to take on your problems, or he would tell you how to solve it! His family was very dependent upon him and he literally took on the role as the Head. If his brothers got in trouble he'd tell them what to do or help get them out of what it was they got themselves into. He would lend money, and not expect to get it back. Most of the time he didn't.

Often times, well, every time his mother had a doctor's appointment he was there to take her. When it came to his mom, he was supportive and dependable. Several occasions on his day off, he would come home late; exhausted from dealing with mom. Not only was she dealing with health issues she was also combating depression and paranoia. She was tormented with these spirits and Edward didn't know how to avoid them being transferred to him. By this, I mean that if you (Believers) don't cover yourselves with daily bread (Word) meditation in his Word, prayer and confession, a tormenting spirit can be transferred. This would occur many times and I would get frustrated when he wouldn't talk, he'd mope around and complain about things so small and insignificant. This drove a wedge between us and was crippling our relationship. Many times we would argue or stop speaking for days at a time. I would stop praying and reading the Word. I began to pray differently. But I found one scripture that wasn't a prayer. How many of you believe the Word?" "Death and life are in the power of the tongue" Proverbs 18:21 KJV. I began to speak out loud the woes that had been bestowed on my husband. For example, he would breathe loudly and chew his food loudly. This began to become really irritating to me. I would go upstairs to our bedroom to speak things openly, such as "I wish he would choke on his food, make him not chew so loudly." This open confession went on for months. I remind you now, that I was a born again, tongue talking, bible toting, Christian woman and mother. My sister Judith told me about the Dirty Harry prayers. I said, what are they? She began to explain to me what they were. Dirty Harry was a Clint Eastwood character that would react on impulse and then ask questions later. He would happily shoot and kill the aggressor without remorse.

One morning Edward and I were eating breakfast and he began to choke on his food. He had just drunk a glass of water. This happened for weeks until he decided to go to the doctor to have it checked out. It just so happened that his food was not being digested, it was stuck in his esophagus. At that time I was friends with a great woman of

God, Mary Rowan, founder and director of Immanuel Missions. I had asked her to agree with me in prayer that God would heal my husband. In her exact words, "Lenora, I had a friend who spoke over her husband the same as you had done! Her husband died." Tears of repentance began falling uncontrollably, I fell on my knees and began to pray out to God; first of all to forgive me for the words I had confessed. I did not know that I was walking in witchcraft. The three spirits of witchcraft are; manipulation, domination and intimidation. I was working all three and my words were manifested when Edward became ill. I also prayed for the healing of my husband. Hear me well; our words have power! It was two weeks later that my husband received his healing. To God be the glory!

I have had pastors to say that if you didn't do a certain thing, or if you went to a certain meeting, they would prophesy that something negative would happen to you. Little did they know that, that was a witchcraft spirit. The witchcraft spirit is merely a spirit in which one desires to have control over another. Don't confuse this with prophesying.

I have often been guilty of this in raising my older sons. For example: my second son Ean had a job interview and had to drive some distance. It was raining and actually I didn't want him to go! So, I simply said, "Well, you don't know where it's located and it's raining; you can easily get lost and be late!" That's exactly what happened. He couldn't find the building, and he turned into a gas station to ask for directions. After getting directions, it began to rain heavily, so he just returned home! I had planted that seed! I used manipulation-intimidation and domination.

The Holy Spirit revealed this to me, I repented, and Ean did get a job a few weeks later.

From that time on I began to confess the Word over my husband and my sons. My husband Edward is a righteous and godly man. He fears God and walks upright. He is a committed father and husband and a righteous example. My sons are godly and men of integrity.

Wives and mothers, if you are familiar with this situation, check your confessions and prayer life, and make sure you confess blessings and life into every one of your situations.

Chapter 7
Let Go and Let GOD!!

Luke 1:31-35

31 And behold, you will conceive in your womb and bring forth a Son, and shall call His name Jesus. 32 He will be great, and will be called the Son of the Highest; and the Lord God will give Him the throne of His father David. 33 And He will reign over the house of Jacob forever, and of His kingdom there will be no end."

34 Then Mary said to the angel, "How can this be, since I do not know a man?"

35 And the angel answered and said to her," The Holy Spirit will come upon you, and the power of the Highest will overshadow you; therefore, also, that Holy One who is to be born will be called the Son of God, NKJV

Let me back up and elaborate for a moment. Mary was a young, Jewish virgin who was engaged to a young man named Joseph, a carpenter by profession. Although Joseph was his earthly father; Jesus had to submit to the authority that Joseph had over him. Now, 'You not my baby daddy' is a cliché that is believed to be derived from the black culture and black single mothers who have had babies by more than one man. This is a culture unto itself. Young girls have convinced themselves that loving a man means having his baby which in turn lets us know that she falls in love a lot, because these young ladies have more than two children.

Many of these young women lead a promiscuous lifestyle and find themselves in said situation. And this is sad because those siblings are raised in biased environments. They have different fathers; some see them, some don't, some know who they are, some of them don't. There are different extended family members - grandparents - aunts, uncles and cousins, some of whom interact in their (blood child's) life some who don't.

It is difficult to grow up in these environments because

so often, the child grows up resenting his parent(s), and therefore turns to the streets for a sense of belonging. That's why the Lord speaks of the covenant of marriage. Two parents can make a difference in a child's life, especially in his/her young formative years. Let's train up our children the way they should go; and when they are older, they will not depart.

I just think about Mary; the mother of Jesus and Joseph as they were raising him while they were young. I'm sure there were times when she had to "put her foot down" and demand his obedience. For example: when Mary and Joseph had taken him to another town, and he went missing for a couple days. Now, you mothers, if you were thinking what I was thinking, "Wait until I find that boy", or close to tears, "where's my baby?" But he was later found in the temple teaching. -Whew, what relief!! A mother's worst nightmare did not occur, but can you imagine her dilemma? What do you think Joseph was thinking? That's my question! "Mary don't fret he'll turn up" or "the boy is twelve years old Mary!!" Now mothers, Mary was human, and a mother now, and I wonder if she was thinking, "Joseph, you not my baby daddy!" God had entrusted her with His Son, and now she's lost him?

Most often women are just thrilled with the idea of being a mother. We don't even ask ourselves these questions: Is he going to be a good father? Will he support his child and will he be in the child's life?

I still have a problem trying to understand why women would put themselves in this position. What position? Not knowing who the father of their child is! Some women grew into adulthood without experiencing healthy parental love. Well, here I go with another cliché, "Looking for love in all the wrong places." You may go to the clubs, the wild concerts, etc. looking for whatever. I've asked myself on several occasions, why do people go to church? The Holy Spirit whispered to me "broken and incomplete people go to the clubs to meet other broken and incomplete people." So it's true? You are frequently in the club to meet someone just like yourself!

The time is now women, ladies, young ladies; to keep yourself with all diligence. We were put here for a purpose. And that purpose is to seek, to knock. Seek the Lord first in all that we do. Ask, "what is my purpose?" When you knock, in sincerity, the door will be opened to you.

In love and respect, get to know the Lord and he will satisfy you, seek his ways and he will lead you into a loving path of righteousness. Love him, and he will show you the love and give you the peace that surpasses all understanding.

Mary knew who the father of her child was, it was God Almighty. Although he was born in a lowly place, He is now seated on the right hand of the Father making intercession (praying) for me. Hallelujah!!

Chapter 8

You Not My Baby Daddy

Read and meditate on the scriptures in this chapter.

When Mary was told by the angel that she was to conceive a child by the Holy Ghost; could you imagine her amazement? Put yourself in her place. Can you just fathom the thoughts and the questions that went through her mind? Why did God choose me? How will all of this come to pass? What an awesome responsibility; yet she received it with faith, obedience and humility.

Often times, we as parents tend to challenge God about our children. By this, I mean that we have the mindset that we know what's best for our children more than God does. We think that we can love better than God, teach better than God, and some of us, even provide better than God. I say to you, "Let Go and Let God."

We serve a merciful and gracious God. He is so faithful

and just. What touches my heart so intensely is that we have brand-new mercies every day. (Lamentations 3:23) We can merely mention his name (Jesus) and he is near. Have you ever thought about the breath that we breathe? Where it comes from? And where it goes when we die?

Know this that God has given unto us all things that pertain to life and godliness. (2 Pet. 1:3). The choices that we make; and the words we speak, are even more crucial than the air that we breathe. Proverbs 18:21 says, "Death and life are in the power of the tongue: and they that love it shall eat the fruit thereof." KJV That lets us know that we must be careful of what we say. Jesus said in John 12:50 "whatsoever I speak therefore, even as the Father said unto me, so I speak." KJV We want prosperity, peace, abundance and healing, we must know what the Word of God says about these things for our lives. For example: if you are experiencing sickness, confess Psalms 103:3. Scripture speaks of healing. I promise you, when you confess with your mouth and say these scriptures every day; watch the healing manifest itself. You must *believe first*. God's Word never fails!! Here are some confessions that I have spoken for years. From Dr. Bridget's Women of the Word Confession. .

"Father in the name of Jesus, this day I will
Delight myself in you. I am in control of my actions,
And I do only those things that please you. I let the word of
God dwell in me richly in all wisdom. I honor my parents and
I look forward to my long days. I excel in everything I put my
hands to do: School work, sports and other activities.
I am an over comer. **I am** more than a conqueror. You live in
me now!!!!
I walk in divine health; sickness and disease has no place in
my body.
I am an obedient child of God, chosen of God and protected
by the Blood of Jesus and healed by His stripes! Amen."

And another one:

"Father, in the name of Jesus, I pray and confess Your Word over my life and I surround myself with faith, faith that you watch over your Word to perform it.

I confess that Jesus loves me, and I cast all my cares on Him. I am the righteousness of God in Christ Jesus. I obey my parents in the Lord and honor them both. I obey and respect those in authority. I am above and not beneath. I confess that I have angels that have charge over me to keep me in All my ways. I surround myself with godly friends. I listen to the voice of the Lord because my steps are ordered by Him. . I speak only those things that uplift and edify and no corrupt communication comes out of my mouth.

I speak the truth at all times and I increase in wisdom and favor with God and man. I walk in divine health I forbid any sickness or disease

To come upon me today. I am submitted to God and the devil flees from me. . . Amen"

I can now understand why it has been so hard for many

mothers and women to allow God to be active in their lives. This is due to our own parents, how we were raised and the words spoken over us.

'Customs and Traditions' this is called soul-ties, or what I call them 'Flesh-Ties!' Either way, they are the all-consuming spirits that have been transferred to us from birth. Our relationships, belief systems and how we function everyday has determined where we are now, spiritually.

Years ago it was too difficult to give God my problems. I was so full of pride, and I didn't want my family to see my vulnerability; but I called it failure. My husband and I were going through some financial stress and we had filed chapter thirteen. It was filed in bankruptcy court. We paid all of our creditors, but we paid them in small amounts. It took about eighteen months, but we were free and clear of debt. (Praise God!) During that time my husband had put me on a strict budget, and I had resorted to finding a cheap seamstress. Excuse me, she was very inexpensive and a really sweet person, which in fact; saved my husband a lot of money in the clothing department.

Long after that time I learned how to stretch; and make do with what I had. I even discovered my creative side, and started adding to my wardrobe by making homemade hats.

It was hard to humble myself; but the Word *does* say to "humble yourself." I began to really listen to my husband; and accept his wise counsel. This made me actually become one with him; in our thinking, praying and one in our agreement in everyday situations.

This was also a period in my life when I began to ask the Lord for humility and a stronger more intense prayer life. Be careful what you ask for. Be it good, bad or indifferent. Life and death is in the power of the tongue, and what you confess with your mouth will come to pass. Solving problems, settling disputes, interceding, laying on of hands, praying, fasting, confessing the Word and just keeping my mouth shut; was the result of Letting Go and Letting God.

www.ingramcontent.com/pod-product-compliance
Lightning Source LLC
LaVergne TN
LVHW020655100826
845148LV00012B/2505